NOT
LEFT
BEHIND

YORKVILLE PRESS

NEW YORK, NEW YORK

www.yorkvillepress.com

LIBRARY OF CONGRESS CATALOGING-IN-PUBLICATION DATA IS ON FILE WITH PUBLISHER

ISBN: 0-9767442-5-2
Printed in Canada

Photography by Troy Snow
Text by Bob Somerville
Design by Tina Taylor

Best Friends
ANIMAL SOCIETY

NOT LEFT BEHIND
Rescuing the Pets of New Orleans

PHOTOGRAPHY BY TROY SNOW
TEXT BY BOB SOMERVILLE

Based on interviews with rescuers Paul Berry, Russ Mead, Troy Snow, Ethan Gurney, Jeff Popowich and Kit Boggio

Dedication

This book is dedicated to all the rescuers, volunteers and donors who did whatever they could, in whatever way their talents allowed, to help save as many as possible of the tens of thousands of pets affected by Hurricane Katrina throughout the Gulf Coast region.

Contents

"THE CITY WAS DEAD CALM. YOU COULD HEAR A SCREEN DOOR SLAPPING IN THE BREEZE EVEN THOUGH IT WAS WAY DOWN THE STREET."

— *Jeff Popowich*

"I AIN'T GOIN' NOWHERE WITHOUT MY BABIES."

— Woman evacuee

"IT WAS ALL EERILY BEAUTIFUL AND DISARMING, AND VERY SAD.
THERE WAS A PROFOUND SADNESS IN ALL THAT SILENCE."

— *Paul Berry*

"SOME ANIMALS HAD BEEN STRANDED FOR CLOSE TO TWO WEEKS WHEN WE GOT TO THEM. SOME WERE ON PORCHES, SOME MAROONED ON CAR HOODS AND ROOFS, DOING WHATEVER THEY COULD TO SURVIVE."

— *Troy Snow*

"YOU'RE GOING THROUGH A NEIGHBORHOOD AND THERE'S NO PEOPLE, NO GRASS, NO BIRDS, NO ANIMALS. . . AND IT'S BEAUTIFUL BUT YOU KNOW HOW SCREWED UP IT IS THAT IT LOOKS THIS WAY, WHAT IT MEANS THAT IT LOOKS THIS WAY."

— *Kit Boggio*

INTRODUCTION

"I JUST HAVE TO TELL THIS STORY."

That's how Best Friends photographer Troy Snow talks about his two weeks with a team of Best Friends rescuers in the New Orleans area helping to save pets in the wake of Hurricane Katrina. *Not Left Behind* is that story, told stunningly, hauntingly, and movingly in the photographs Troy took during those two weeks.

One of the many tragedies associated with Katrina was that most evacuees had to leave their pets behind, a wrenching experience that was more heartbreaking for many than losing their homes. Paul Berry, executive director of Best Friends and a native of New Orleans, got to the area the day after the storm hit and began the process of setting up a "temporary" rescue center at the St. Francis Animal Sanctuary in Tylertown, Mississippi, about one hundred miles north of New Orleans. As it turned out, that temporary center remained in operation for more than eight months.

St. Francis itself had been badly hit, and needed emergency power, water and food for the animals. Back in Utah, Troy and three other Best Friends colleagues—Russ Mead, Ethan Gurney and Jeff Popowich—loaded up trucks and trailers with supplies and started driving. They had generators, food, dog collars, leashes and catchpoles, as well as crates, fencing and anything else they could think of, including tarpaulins, twist ties and duct tape. Troy brought along two cameras, one for a zoom lens and one for wide angle.

With two dogs aboard, Ethan Gurney, Jeff Popowich and photographer Troy Snow (left to right) head in from one of their countless rescue missions through the flooded streets of New Orleans. (For the story of the two dogs shown here, see pages 40-45.)

(Photograph by Leah Hogsten, Salt Lake Tribune)

Some three hundred miles from what would be home base at Tylertown, they began to see signs of the hurricane's destruction. At one stop, they met a woman who had partitioned her car into several compartments with chicken wire. She had two dogs in one area, five cats in another section, and a bird in a third part of the car. She had driven out of New Orleans before the storm hit and strung up the chicken wire to make a rudimentary ark for her precious pets. "I had to. They're my babies," she said. "I just couldn't leave them behind."

Troy and the others spent their first night at the St. Francis sanctuary sleeping on the ground. The next day, Russ, who would be coordinating the setup there, Ethan and Jeff began building runs and figuring out what else was needed. People were always ready to help. On one trip for supplies, they got some help finding what they needed from a woman customer who knew her way around. When they got to checkout, there she was, credit card in hand: She paid for the several hundred dollars' worth of supplies and waved off their thanks. "It's the least I can do."

Eventually, Troy, Jeff and Ethan made their way down to the city, where they met up with Paul and other Best Friends teams. Troy took pictures but mostly he helped with the rescues, which lasted from first light to last. "I didn't really have a case of the photojournalist's dilemma—do I take pictures or help," he recalls. "Actually, more often than not, I had to remind myself to pick up the camera and take some pictures, there was just so much else to do."

Some of what they experienced in the next two weeks is detailed in the photographs that fill this book. But they and many others did so much more. Best Friends was the first animal rescue organization to hit the flooded streets, but there were ultimately many others involved as well. The unprecedented scope of the storm was in key ways matched by an unprecedented response at the grassroots level—from rescuers on the scene and thousands of supporters and donors around the country.

Not Left Behind doesn't attempt to provide a complete picture of what was done to rescue the pets of New Orleans. Probably no single book ever can. But in its small way, the story of what these few did speaks volumes about the spirit of compassion that floated on those waters of destruction.

As for the animals shown on these pages, they too represent but a few of literally tens of thousands of pets affected by the catastrophe. Their expressions also speak volumes—telling of fear and desperation and despair, but also of hope and resilience. Many of these animals were ultimately reunited with their families; almost all of the rest found new homes. There were indeed many many happy endings.

As a national community, we made mistakes in responding to Katrina. But we also did things right. In our ignorance, we insisted that people leave without their pets. But in our compassion we went back, and we made sure that as many as possible were, in the end, NOT LEFT BEHIND.

OPPOSITE: *Paul Berry grips the wheel and Kit Boggio, one of the Best Friends team, rides shotgun on the daily trip from Tylertown to New Orleans. "The windshield washer fluid was practically useless against the bug splatter," says Paul. "I just got used to seeing through the muck."*

LEFT: *Paul compares notes with a member of the 82nd Airborne at a staging area. Frontline military personnel helped animal rescuers locate dogs the troops had seen stranded in the flooded parts of the city.*

OBSTACLES AND ALLIES

Just getting to New Orleans was an ordeal for the Best Friends team. Their base at Tylertown was about two hours away, and the whole journey had a surreal quality. The devastation got worse mile by mile, the roads harder to negotiate, and endless lines snaked away from every open gas station. "It was like a scene out of *Mad Max*," says Troy. "You couldn't believe what you were seeing."

Roadblocks were an exercise in persuasiveness for Paul Berry. In those early days, nothing got done except by those who just went in and did it, and Paul was the master at making that possible. Though there were a few dicey moments on occasion, Best Friends vehicles never got turned away.

In New Orleans itself, Paul was soon coordinating with the military personnel who were running rescue missions into the flooded parts of the city. He arranged for Troy and Jeff and Ethan to go along, scoping out where there might be animals to save, while he managed to procure two or three boats for their own use. Officialdom itself was Paul's new roadblock and called for some stealthy resourcefulness. "While rescue officials argued over who was in charge of which bureaucracy," says Paul, "we'd sneak our boats in and do rescues."

It wasn't the same with the frontline military guys: They were only too eager to help. To them it was a no-brainer that animal rescuers should be right in there getting that part of the job done.

RIGHT: *Mardi Gras beads hang from a tree blown over by Katrina's winds.*

FAR RIGHT: *Major Townley Hedrick of the 82nd Airborne reaches out to a just-rescued dog. "These guys cared as much as we did," says Troy.*

Spray-painted code marks a building that has been checked by the military. To the left and right of the X are the date and time of the inspection. At top is the designation for the military company. The bottom quadrant was originally used to note any dead bodies on the premises, but some patrols started adding a second number to indicate the presence of any living pets.

Alabama Kenny

"Alabama Kenny, awesome guy," says Kit, recalling a key member of the volunteer team. Kenny, like so many of those who wanted to do whatever they could, just showed up at Tylertown one day early on. He had taken vacation time from his job at an animal shelter and was asking what he could do to help. Somebody mentioned the need for more boats for the rescue teams. "I have a boat," said Kenny. "I'll get it and be back tomorrow."

No one realized that Kenny lived in Pell City, Alabama, about 300 miles from Tylertown and a five-hour drive at the best of times.

Kenny was back the following day with his johnboat after an overnight trip of more than 600 miles. He joined the next convoy of Best Friends vehicles heading down to the city and was soon out on the water rescuing dogs. (Kenny is looking back toward the camera in the picture above.)

> "THEIR EYES SEEMED TO BE SAYING TO ME,
> 'WHAT AM I DOING HERE? AND WHERE ARE MY PEOPLE?'"
>
> —*Troy Snow*

The Jefferson Parish Shelter

Before the Best Friends team got out on the water on their own, they spent several days ferrying already-rescued pets from the Jefferson Parish shelter, an official city facility, to the St. Francis Animal Sanctuary in Tylertown. It was clear to Troy that most of these animals had never seen the inside of a shelter before: "Their eyes seemed to be saying to me, 'Where am I? And where are my people?'" Picking up animals at Jefferson became part of the daily routine even when the team was bringing in pets directly from the streets. Many rescue organizations eventually established similar ferrying-out operations.

RESCUES

Out on their own in Kenny's boat, Ethan, Jeff and Troy began searching for animals to rescue. "We would go into a neighborhood and do our best to stay where the roads were so we wouldn't hit something," Troy recalls. "We'd call out and make barking noises and shout, 'Here, boy!' or 'Want a treat?' Then we'd shut the motor off and just float down the street, listening really carefully. When we heard a dog barking, we'd head in that direction." But that didn't always mean they could find the dog, at least not right away. "We thought we heard barking inside this building," says Ethan, "but it turned out it was coming from an alleyway in the back that was flooded and clogged with debris. And this miniature poodle was trapped in the alley, struggling to hold his head out of the water by propping his front paws up on a piece of steel frame." They clambered in and got the dog out. Days later, after a good bath at Tylertown, the little gray poodle they had rescued turned out to be white as snow.

Ethan peers into a locked building looking for a dog they'd heard barking (opposite). The little gray miniature poodle they found in the back (left) had been trying to stay above the floodwaters for days.

Help from Above

"We were really excited," recalls Jeff of his first day in the city with Ethan doing rescues. "We had stopped to talk to a couple of media guys, and they told us about this dog in a boat near an on ramp. We could see her from above, and there were a couple of dead bodies in the water. The water wasn't very deep, but to get to that dog, we had to walk between those bodies. And all I could think was, I don't want to slip, I don't want to slip." When they got to the boat, they found the dog tied loosely with a piece of rope, and Jeff picked her up and carried her back. "As we were walking up the ramp, all these media people started clapping. But we didn't really do anything they couldn't have done."

"EVERY DAY, WHEN YOU GOT THAT FIRST ANIMAL, I DIDN'T CARE WHAT ELSE HAPPENED. AS LONG AS YOU GOT THAT FIRST ONE, IT WAS A GOOD DAY."

—*Jeff Popowich*

A soldier reaches out to pet Goldie, safe in Ethan's arms. "Some guys were running low on food for themselves from feeding the dogs," says Ethan. "I was just dumbfounded at what they did for the animals."

Goldie

As they were cruising the city's flooded streets, the Best Friends teams occasionally came upon sections of higher ground, almost like islands. One of these spots was a local military base that had been evacuated before the storm; the departing troops had parked military vehicles at the entrance to block the gates. That's where Ethan found Goldie. "She was just lying there, completely listless," he remembers. "She was badly dehydrated and suffering from the heat, and she seemed sick, perhaps from trying to drink dirty water." Ethan got her to safety and she soon recovered. As always, the military folks were just as happy to see an animal rescued. "Our biggest asset was the military," says Ethan. "They'd come find us and tell us where animals were. They were collecting dogs themselves, keeping as many as 30 dogs together in fenced areas. They were breaking all the rules—but it was working out just fine."

"SHE WAS COMPLETELY LISTLESS WHEN I FOUND HER,
BUT SHE RECOVERED WELL WHEN WE GOT HER TO SAFETY."

—*Ethan Gurney*

Pals on the Brink

"We sometimes came upon two dogs together," recalls Troy. "We wondered at first if that might make things more difficult, but in general it meant we could bring back more animals in one boatload." The johnboats they were using could typically hold either two dogs that had to be kept apart or three if two of them were pals.

The two dogs shown here and on the following pages were perched on the edge of an almost fully submerged boat still on its trailer in the driveway. They had probably been there for close to two weeks when Jeff, Ethan and Troy found them. "You could tell as we approached that they were happy to see us," Troy remembers. "But you could also tell they were in pretty bad shape." As the following pages detail, rescue sometimes called for immediate medical care.

Jeff eases the boat in past debris while Ethan prepares to bring the healthier-looking dark dog aboard. Both animals were starving and dehydrated.

SHE WAS OBVIOUSLY NERVOUS—WE WERE STRANGERS, AFTER ALL.
BUT AS SOON AS I PICKED HER UP, SHE JUST MELTED IN MY ARMS."

—*Jeff Popowich*

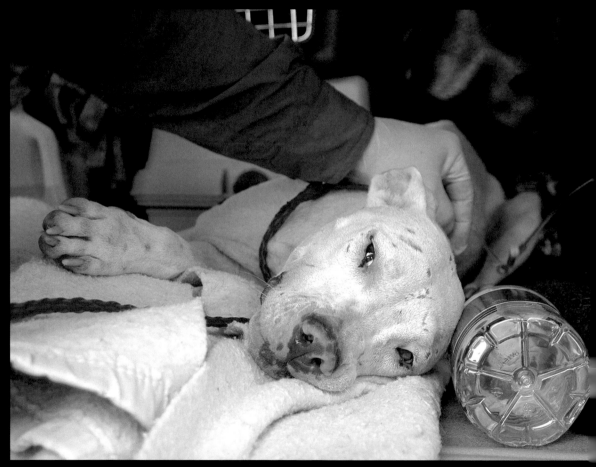

After getting both animals on the boat, Ethan and Jeff decide the dogs need to be taken right away to the staging area at the water's edge. In the back of the SUV, veterinarian Dr. Debbie Rykoff prepares to administer intravenous liquids, choosing the dark dog first because he seems to have a better chance of making it. The white dog is too weak to hold up her head, but within moments of getting the IV, she begins to perk up (opposite).

Kenny hands the two rescued cats out to Kit. "I held onto them for the rest of the time, just held them and loved them."

Hard to See, Hard to Rescue

The difference between cats and dogs was stark in the flooded neighborhoods. You could call for dogs and they would answer, and come to you if they could. But cats broke the rescuers' hearts time and again, dashing off out of sight, or showing up tantalizingly on a rooftop out of reach. That's what made Kit Boggio's first rescue a special one. "This house had all its windows open," she recalls, "and I saw these two cats sitting in one of the windows, looking out and waiting." They pulled up the boat, Kenny climbed in through a window, and soon Kit had them. "It felt really good to get those cats. I didn't rescue any others." Later on, a trapping strategy using food for bait enabled Best Friends to rescue more than a thousand cats.

"THOSE CATCHPOLES WERE LIFESAVERS. WE WOULDN'T HAVE BEEN ABLE TO SAVE HALF THE DOGS WE DID WITHOUT THEM."

—*Jeff Popowich*

Jeff and Ethan use catchpoles—stiff tubes with a rope loop on the end—to handle two difficult dogs. "They give you a lot better control," Jeff notes, "and helped protect both us and other dogs from getting bitten."

Not Left Behind

Rescues in the city typically went on until the last light of the day, when it was time to take all the rescued animals up to Tylertown. But one day, the Best Friends team got a very clear message that it wasn't quite time to leave. "We were wrapping up for the day," says Jeff, "loading the boat up, pulling it out of the water, putting it on the trailer, getting all the dogs loaded up on the truck—and we hear one more dog crying. We knew he was close just by the sound. When you hear this one dog in a dead city, there's no mistaking it, and it's heartbreaking, and you can't let it go. We all just looked at each other, got the boat, put it in the water, and went to get him." The dog was in the back of a trailer, and someone had built a makeshift shelter for him out of hay bales. "So this skinny little hound was sitting there, and we just picked him up and put him in the boat and turned around and went back."

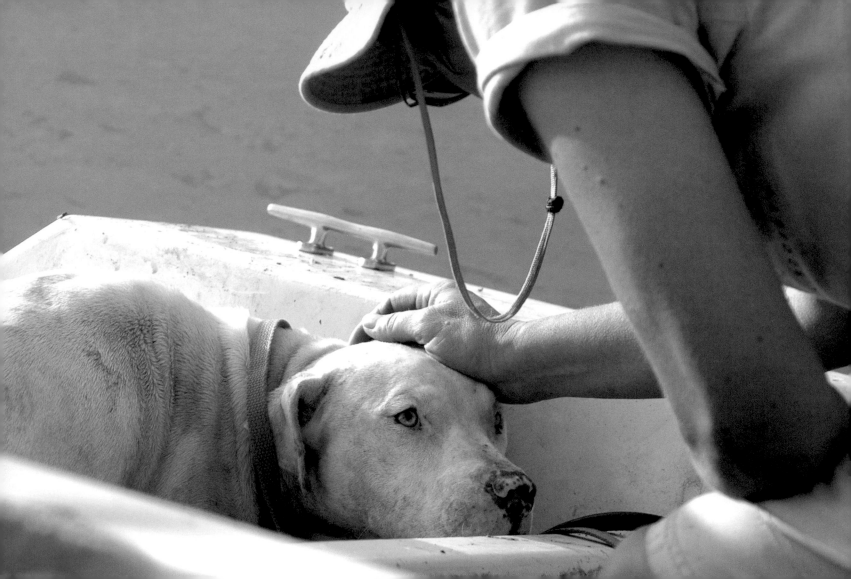

"I PICKED HER UP AND HELD HER AND LOOKED AT PAUL—I REMEMBER LOOKING AT HIM, AND THE THOUGHT IN MY HEAD WAS, CAN YOU BELIEVE THIS?"

—*Kit Boggio*

"SHE SEEMED FRIGHTENED TO THE POINT OF SHOCK AND IMMOBILITY. WHEN I GOT HER IN MY ARMS SHE WAS QUITE STIFF. WE DIDN'T KNOW WHAT WE WERE IN FOR WITH HER, WHETHER SHE WAS EVEN GOING TO MAKE IT."

—*Paul Berry*

Dog in Boat

Paul Berry did his share of rescues, along with coordinating the Best Friends teams and assessing where needs were the greatest. One day, he ran into some military folks who told him there was a dog in a boat right down at the end of one of the main highways that runs into New Orleans. "They didn't say if it was alive or dead, just that they'd seen this dog in a boat," Paul remembers. He, Kit Boggio and Troy hopped into the truck and drove down the interstate to where the flooding began, and there was a boat washed up by the side of the road, spray-painted with unmistakable directions: DOG IN BOAT (see pages 52-53).

Paul held the boat steady while Kit climbed up and in. "There was this dog huddled down in the back by the motor," she recalls, "and there was water underneath her, and she was all sunburned and covered in this thick goo. That's why I named her Diesel." Kit handed Diesel to Paul; they wrapped her in a blanket, got her back to one of the staging areas, and got critical care started right away. She was up in Tylertown that night. "It was amazing," Kit recalls, "how after three or four days of resting and eating and getting fluids she came around. Her sunburn blisters went away, and her pads were healing, and there she was."

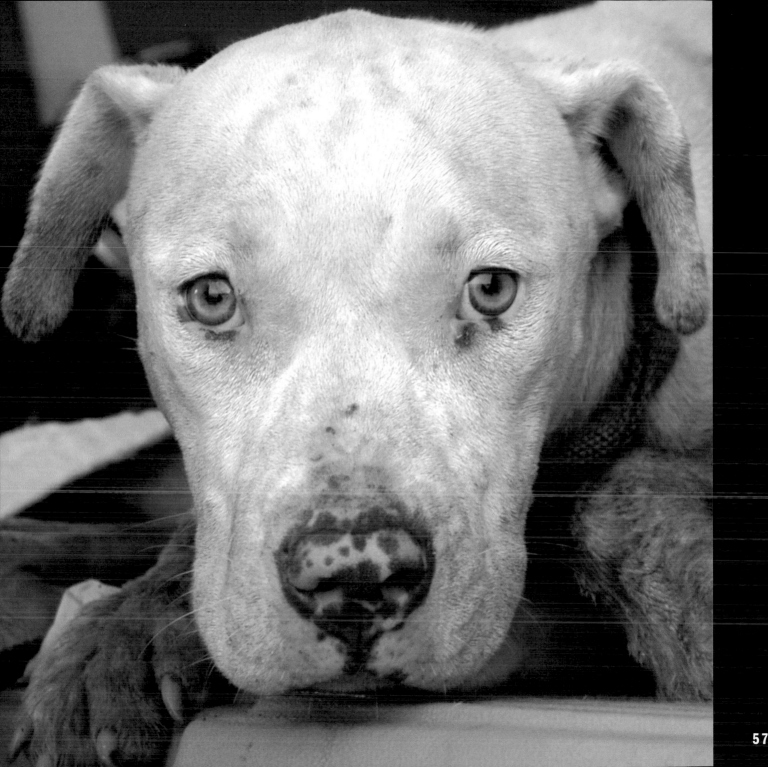

Swimming for Help

"This is one of those rescues I'll never forget," recalls Troy. "Like everybody else, I had my own stereotypes about pit bulls, so I was a little nervous when we saw these two on top of an almost fully submerged car. And then one of them jumped into the water and started swimming right at us. You could see by his eyes that he was a little confused, but he definitely wanted to get to us. I didn't know if he was coming to say, Get out of my territory, or if he was coming for help. I took a picture of him as he swam toward me, and then this big old pit bull head is staring up at me, on my side of the boat. I put down my camera, took a deep breath, then reached down and just grabbed this dog and pulled him up into the boat."

It was an anxious moment for Troy, but his fears were soon allayed. "He was just nuzzling his head into my neck, and his tail was just thumping against the side of the boat, just thumping so loud, bam bam bam bam. He would have climbed right inside of you. This dog had been trapped on the roof of a car in his own driveway, no clean water, no food, waiting for his owners to come back. He's sunburned. He's sick. But the most important thing in that dog's life right then was being loved. He couldn't get close enough to me."

After they rescued the first dog, Jeff maneuvered the boat in and they picked up his companion (pages 60-61).

"SHE WAS A LITTLE FREAKED OUT, BUT SHE WAS ALSO EXCITED TO SEE US, AND EXTREMELY HAPPY TO BE WITH US WHEN WE GOT HER ON BOARD."

—Jeff Popowich

As the Waters Recede...

In the course of the two weeks that Troy was in New Orleans taking pictures, the floodwaters began to recede.
The Best Friends rescuers could see the progress of the waters going down, almost like the striated layers of red rock
back home in Utah. But it actually didn't make things any easier. "We went from boat rescues to boat-land rescues,"
says Paul. "We would start hitting dry spots by the end of the day. We would have to get out, wade through the water,
carry the boats over, and then get moving again." And the rescues went on and on. The little black puppy shown
above was found by the team near City Hall, just at the edge of the water where the military had one of its main
staging areas. "The soldiers had been feeding him scraps," says Troy, "and then we found him, and Dr. Deb picked
him up, wrapped him in a blanket and set him on the seat of the truck." She later adopted him.

"THE CITY HAD NEVER COMPLETELY FLOODED LIKE THAT, SO A LOT OF PEOPLE'S REACTION PROBABLY WAS, WE HAVE TO EVACUATE, BUT WE'LL BE BACK IN A FEW DAYS. WE'LL JUST LEAVE THE DOG IN THE BACKYARD, GIVE HIM EXTRA WATER AND A BIG BOWL OF FOOD, AND WE'LL BE BACK IN A FEW DAYS..."

—*Jeff Popowich*

TYLERTOWN

Russ Mead, Ethan, Jeff and Troy had driven out from Best Friends Animal Sanctuary in southern Utah to Tylertown—a journey of nearly 2,000 miles—loaded down with a wide assortment of supplies. "We took what we thought we would need," Russ remembers, "although the scope of Katrina was so massive that there was no way we could have taken all the materials we ultimately required. But we took fencing, posthole drivers, various other tools, generators, leashes and catchpoles and collars and crates—and a lot of pet food." It turned out to be one of the few missteps on the supply side of things. "What ended up happening was that virtually every group that came to help would bring food, and delivery trucks kept showing up—about every 45 minutes during that first week—loaded with at least half a ton of pet food each. We eventually had to rent a huge warehouse just to store all the food we had. It was very much a loaves-and-fishes phenomenon." The miracle of generosity from donors and volunteers that lies at the heart of everything Best Friends does was clearly working overtime at Tylertown.

Jeff and Ethan deliver a young pup to the Best Friends shelter at Tylertown. The tag attached to his collar includes crucial information about where the dog was found. Such data ultimately helped Best Friends reunite many pets with their families.

The St. Francis Animal Sanctuary in Tylertown was a fledgling operation—only a few buildings and a staff of four—that Best Friends had helped establish in 2000. Once the Best Friends team got to the 38-acre property, they began right away constructing runs for the animals who would soon be arriving from New Orleans. Russ fell into the role of organizing the setup effort. "We were bringing in up to 70 dogs and cats and other animals every night," says Paul. "And every day Russ woud build out more capacity to accommodate the new arrivals. He did this for three weeks straight, with hardly any sleep, building new runs all day and helping with new arrivals all night. He never once lost his smile and his enthusiasm. He kept us all going."

At the end of a day of building, the volunteers would grab something to eat and try to nap for an hour before the rescue team returned. "We'd finish building runs at about 10 o'clock at night," Russ remembers, "and the dogs would arrive at midnight. Between then and about three in the morning we unloaded the crates and walked the dogs, and they spent the night in this area we had set aside for the new arrivals. The next morning we would look at the paperwork that came with them, we would microchip every animal and then we would take care of any medical needs that hadn't been handled right away on a critical care basis. Somebody called the arrivals area Ellis Island, and the name stuck."

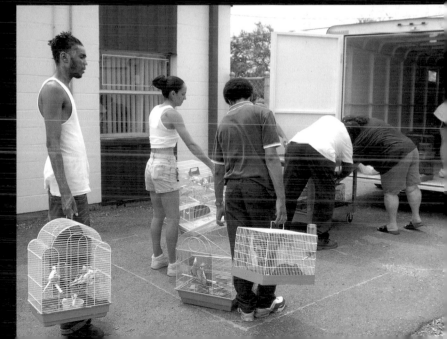

BELOW: *Volunteers load birds and other animals rescued from a local pet store onto a truck for shipment to Tylertown. Openings in the trailer were hacksawed by the volunteers to provide ventilation in the sweltering heat.*

The animals were then assigned to different locations around the sanctuary as appropriate. Smaller dogs to what became known as Toytown, larger ones to Pooch Alley, and cats to sections of the three already-existing buildings at the St. Francis sanctuary. The burgeoning dog runs—eventually with a capacity of up to 600 dogs—turned out to be one of the better ideas the Best Friends team put into effect. "We didn't have a lot of prior experience in open-water rescue," Russ laughs, "but we do animal care and sheltering very well. These displaced pets were totally traumatized. We couldn't just put them in the traditional crates used in animal rescue. They needed a real sanctuary. The big outdoor runs were much easier on the dogs. And another thing is that the other groups who relied on crates needed tons of volunteers just to walk the dogs. Because we invested in a sanctuary-type environment, our volunteers were able to focus on critical life-saving work."

Jeff and Ethan unload some of the very first dogs to arrive at the St. Francis sanctuary from New Orleans. Crates were used almost exclusively for transport; volunteers built more dog runs every day to keep ahead of the increasing numbers of animals arriving from the city. These little fellows will soon be housed in the area of the sanctuary that came to be known as Toytown.

"IF I WAS DOING THIS AGAIN, I WOULD TAKE ONLY ONE BAG OF PET FOOD, EVEN IF I KNEW I HAD TO FEED 4,000 ANIMALS."

—*Russ Mead*

LEFT: *Best Friends staff and volunteers man a bucket brigade to unload one of the many supply trucks that kept arriving, almost on an hourly basis. "It was a team concept," says Russ, "and I made it clear that there were only two basic rules: Do the most important thing that needs to happen next, and don't do anything stupid. Beyond that, I didn't give them much direction at all. It was up to them to figure out what needed to be done."*

RIGHT: *Unsolicited donations of supplies such as carrying crates and pet food pile up. "We eventually had to rent a huge warehouse to store all the food we had," recalls Russ. "It was very much a loaves-and-fishes phenomenon."*

A volunteer takes one of the rescued dogs for a walk, while another lucky fellow enjoys the unleashed freedom of a run. Having the dogs in runs kept them calmer than they would have been in crates and made walks a matter of pleasure rather than necessity.

LEFT: *One of the cats at Tylertown gets a checkup. Both dogs and cats in particularly bad shape were flown out to specialists for more intensive medical treatment.*

OPPOSITE: *A standard poodle gets a thorough clipping. Volunteer groomers spent as much as 16 hours a day taking care of dogs whose coats were matted with filth. Their expert handling kept the animals calm.*

Getting Ready for a New Lease on Life

As the Tylertown sanctuary evolved, areas were set aside specifically for health care and grooming. Kit Boggio, a nurse by training, helped coordinate the volunteers who had come to attend to the animals' medical needs, including more than half a dozen vets. She also kept her eye on the health of all the volunteers, watching for signs of heat exhaustion, which was a constant concern, and for emotional strain as well. "Kit would take one look at you, even from a distance," Troy remembers, "and then say, 'Hey, get over here. You need a hug.'"

SOME OF THE ANIMALS WERE IN PRETTY BAD SHAPE, AND A FEW DIDN'T MAKE IT. BUT FOLLOWING THE BEST FRIENDS PHILOSOPHY, THE TEAM WOULD GO TO GREAT LENGTHS TO GIVE AN ANIMAL A CHANCE.

"We were sending dogs to specialists," Russ recalls, "having them flown out. If an animal could be saved, we would make sure it happened. We paid for orthopedic surgeons to rebuild dogs' shattered legs, for example. Some offsite vets would do it for free, and some wouldn't, but to us it didn't matter. Whatever the animals needed, the animals got."

Grooming was important both for health reasons and for the animals' own sense of well-being. Some volunteers took charge of bathing the dogs, and there were professional groomers who showed up as well. "I remember one dog groomer in particular," says Russ, "who would take these animals that were matted with tar and all kinds of nasty stuff, to the point where they would have to be shaved to the skin. And of course these dogs were scared, and the clippers were scary, but she could hold her hand on a particular place on the body and get the animal to move exactly as she needed, and somehow the dog would know that she was there to help."

It didn't take a photographer's eye to notice that a good bath, a haircut and a brushing or blow-dry could make a world of difference for these dogs. "You could almost see the fear and anxiety wash away with each loving touch," says Troy. For more than a few of Katrina's four-legged victims, it was a big step toward a new lease on life.

The white pit bull who had seemed so close to death's door right after rescue (inset) still shows signs of emotional trauma as she gets a bath to try to wash off the oily grime of New Orleans' floodwaters. But many of the animals clearly enjoyed getting a chance to look pretty again (opposite and following pages).

"THEY ARE UNCONDITIONALLY LOVING.
MANY OF THESE DOGS CAME FROM POOR
SITUATIONS, BUT WITH A LITTLE LOVING CARE
THEY TURNED AROUND—YOU COULD SEE IT.
THEY WERE ALL GOOD, HONEST DOGS."

—Kit Boggio

All About the Babies

"My jaw would drop when I realized the skill sets we had available," recalls Russ, who screened most of the volunteers showing up day by day and week by week. "I would listen to their background and then assign them into specific areas. Someone who was an engineer, for example, I'd put in charge of a building crew. We even had a genuine rocket scientist, who had taken time off from designing missile guidance systems. He helped me set up a database for keeping track of the animals. There were all sorts of people like that."

Some of the volunteers contributed by keeping the humans healthy and happy. "We had about 75 volunteers there at any one time, and feeding them all was a challenge," says Russ. "Sometimes we had to scramble, but every so often we'd have professional chefs who would come for a week or so and, cooking on a mobile kitchen and working with basic ingredients, would put together gourmet meals for us—off the scale fantastic!" Others opened up their wallets and pocketbooks—quite literally—to serve the cause. "This one woman could tell we needed some help moving materials around, so she gives me the keys to her truck. As I'm thanking her for letting us borrow it, she reaches into her purse, pulls out the title, and hands it over to me."

Some of the most valuable volunteers were those who were just plain good at working with animals. "We had some fantastic animal handlers," Russ recalls. "We had people who could calm the animals down merely by talking to them. These dogs were scared, and of course they were missing their people. So we'd let our best handlers be with them one on one, and they'd get them to a place where they could relax enough to eat and sleep and receive medical care."

"I'm very proud of the work we all did together down there," says Kit. But she hastens to add that at its core the experience was an exercise in selflessness. "There was no 'self' there. There was only this huge task, and these lives to be saved. It wasn't about us at all. It was all about the babies."

Melissa Autin, who joined the Best Friends staff after volunteering at the Tylertown sanctuary, gives some extra loving to a pit bull. She was one of the several caregivers who had a special way with the animals and helped them reclaim their natural joy in life.

Outcomes: Reunions

Aggie Liccriadi was lucky to get out of her New Orleans home, climbing out of a second-floor window because the rest of her house was flooded. She had her beloved golden retriever, Baby, with her, but she thought her luck had turned when she had to leave Baby behind as she herself was evacuated. Five times Aggie was moved to different shelters, each time feeling that her chances of ever finding Baby again were fading. But the best luck of all happened two weeks later, when Aggie managed to get to Tylertown, found Baby, and clutched her tight. "I lost all my possessions," says Aggie, "but the only thing I cared about in the world was Baby, so I haven't lost anything."

A ritual evolved at Tylertown to celebrate such reunions. "Someone would take an old pot and a spoon and would beat on it, and it would make this sound like a gong," says Russ. "Everybody would gather around. People took pictures, and folks were crying, and it was always a big thing. It was important to do, to say there was good that was coming out of all the effort. This was a way of saying yeah, it's all good."

Outcomes: Adoptions

Goldie, who was rescued by Ethan from an evacuated military base in New Orleans, was one of the animals who ended up at Best Friends Animal Sanctuary in Utah. She had the typical happy life of a Best Friends resident, and was rather famous to boot, having appeared on the cover of Best Friends' magazine. As a result, Goldie came to the attention of Marianne Baugher, who with her husband already had four dogs at home. But now they had to have one more. Marianne came out to Utah as soon as she could, and in March of 2006, she adopted Goldie and took her back to Maryland, to their 10-acre property complete with a stream. Sometimes the best home of all is a new one.

Outcomes: Not Left Behind

It doesn't take an expert to see what care and love can do. The little hound mix who called Ethan, Jeff and Troy back for one more rescue at the end of a very long day (pages 50-51) recovered quickly in Tylertown. Like so many others of the more than 3,000 pets that came through Tylertown, he found his inherent joy in life again. The Best Friends temporary sanctuary at Tylertown remained in operation for 249 days, finally closing down in May of 2006. By that time, all the animals had either been reunited with their people, been placed in new homes, or had been brought back to Best Friends for special care. Not one of them was left behind.

"THERE'S OBVIOUSLY A LOT OF SADNESS AND A LOT OF BAD MEMORIES, BUT MORE THAN 3,200 ANIMALS CAME THROUGH TYLERTOWN. THAT TO ME IS AMAZING, THAT A BUNCH OF PEOPLE WERE ABLE TO GO DOWN THERE AND SAVE ALL THOSE PETS."

—*Jeff Popowich*

AFTERWORD BY MICHAEL MOUNTAIN

Michael Mountain, President of Best Friends Animal Society, with Nikko (front) and Vivian.

We call them disasters. And they certainly are.

But in the greater scheme of things, they are also the natural processes of destruction and creation, death and rebirth, ruin and renewal.

Our planet itself was born in violence and upheaval. Without the huge cataclysms of its birth pangs, there would be no life at all.

One of those—a catastrophic event that brought death and destruction to the dinosaurs 65 million years ago—opened the door to the rise of the mammals, including, eventually, us humans.

Fire, flood, wind, and earthquake are still part of the natural order. And Hurricane Katrina brought that fact into stark relief with pain and suffering on an unprecedented scale. But it also gave rise to an unprecedented outpouring of kindness and concern. All across the nation, people reached out to help. Never before had so many people joined together in the simple understanding that people's pets are part of their family—not just things that could and should be abandoned.

In a national poll commissioned by Best Friends in 2006, more than 90 percent of people said that we have a moral obligation to protect the animals in our care. Clearly kindness to animals has moved into the mainstream of the national agenda as federal and local authorities now scramble to change their policies to reflect the will of the people.

Once again, out of the darkness and chaos of destruction, a new light was shining.

Sooner or later, disaster will strike again—either natural or man-made. It will be a powerful force. But we may be witnessing the birth of an even greater force ... the greatest one of all ... the kindness and caring that grow out of the knowledge that we are all one creation, all part of the same fabric of life.

And that would be the greatest rebirth of all.

Sherry Woodard, Best Friends' dog training expert, gets a pooch smooch from Sheriff, one of the dogs rescued from New Orleans and now living at the Best Friends sanctuary in Utah.

Best Friends
ANIMAL SOCIETY

ABOUT BEST FRIENDS ANIMAL SOCIETY
A better world through kindness to animals

Best Friends had its origins in the late 1970s when a group of friends would visit local humane societies to help the homeless pets who were least likely to be adopted. They created a small sanctuary for them, which led in turn to the founding of Best Friends Animal Society.

Today, Best Friends is at the heart of a grassroots movement to bring an end to the killing of homeless pets in shelters and to transform the way people relate to the animals, to nature and to each other.

Best Friends Animal Sanctuary, at the heart of the Golden Circle of southern Utah, is the nation's largest sanctuary for companion animals— home on any given day to about 1,500 dogs, cats and other animals from all over the country and beyond. Many of them need just a few weeks of special care before they're ready to go to good new homes. Others who need long-term care find a permanent home at the sanctuary for the rest of their lives. Thousands of people visit the sanctuary every year to spend their vacation with the animals and in the surrounding national parks.

Best Friends works with humane societies and rescue groups to build community spay/neuter and adoption programs so that every healthy dog or cat who's ever born can be guaranteed a loving home. And through the Best Friends Network online, thousands of people work together to care for animals in their own neighborhoods, in emergencies and in areas of common interest.

The work of Best Friends is supported entirely through the donations of members.

How you can help

- **Become a part of Best Friends.** You can sponsor one of the cats, dogs, or other animals who live at the sanctuary, or just donate to the work of the society.
- **Volunteer at the sanctuary.** Join us for a day or a week or longer. You can walk dogs, groom cats, feed horses, and much more.
- **Help in hundreds of other ways through the Best Friends Network.** See our web site for more information.
- **Adopt an animal from Best Friends or your local shelter.**
- **Make sure your own pets are spayed or neutered.**

How you can contact us

Best Friends Animal Society
5001 Angel Canyon Road
Kanab, Utah 84741

www.bestfriends.org
info@bestfriends.org
(435) 644-2001

(Photograph by Molly Wald)

About the photographer

Troy Snow has been with Best Friends since 2002 and has been one of their photographers since 2003. He lives in Kanab, Utah, with his wife, Vera, daughter, Agnessa, and their two dogs, Lulu (left) and Mellow.